BROOKLANDS
CRADLE OF BRITISH MOTOR RACING AND AVIATION

Nicholas H. Lancaster

SHIRE PUBLICATIONS

Published in Great Britain in 2013 by Shire Publications
Ltd, Midland House, West Way, Botley, Oxford OX2 0PH,
United Kingdom.
43-01 21st St, Suite 220B, Long Island City, NY 11101,
USA.

E-mail: shire@shirebooks.co.uk   www.shirebooks.co.uk

A CIP catalogue record for this book is available from the
British Library.

Shire Library no. 484   •   ISBN 978 0 74780 707 0

Nicholas H. Lancaster has asserted his right under the
Copyright, Designs and Patents Act, 1988, to be identified
as the author of this book.

Designed by Ken Vail Graphic Design, Cambridge, UK and
typeset in Perpetua and Gill Sans.
Originated by PDQ Digital Media Solutions ·
Printed in China through Worldprint

13 14 15 16 17   13 12 11   10 9 8 7 6 5 4

COVER IMAGE
The opening of the Campbell Circuit allowed the BARC to
advertise road racing at last. Aware of competition from
the new circuit in the grounds of the Crystal Palace, the
Campbell Circuit was the Brooklands response as road
racing grew in popularity.

TITLE PAGE IMAGE
An Aero Club brochure, c. 1930, a typical design from that
era that successfully combined the two activities identified
with the name 'Brooklands'.

CONTENTS PAGE IMAGE
Detail of a Brooklands poster from the 1930s.

ACKNOWLEDGEMENTS
The author gratefully acknowledges the assistance of John
Pulford, Head of Collections and Interpretations,
Brooklands Museum; Graham Skillen and Tony Hutchings
of the Brooklands Society; Michael Worthington-Williams,
Peter Heilbron, John Carlton; and Nick Wright and his
colleagues at Shire Publications.

Photographs are acknowledged as follows:

National Motor Museum, page 6; Imperial War Museum,
page 16; Getty Images, pages 24 and 44; Michael
Worthington-Williams, page 27 (bottom); Sammy Davis
Archives, pages 45 (top) and 48 (bottom); John Pulford,
page 50 (bottom); BAE Systems per Brooklands Museum,
pages 22, 23 (bottom), 54 and 57–61; the author, page 62.
All other photographs and illustrations are courtesy of the
Brooklands Museum Trust.

Shire Publications is supporting the Woodland Trust, the UK's leading woodland conservation charity, by funding the dedication of trees.

CONTENTS

BROOKLANDS

5th INTERNATIONAL

500 MILES RACE

SATURDAY

SEPT. 16

STARTING at 11 A.M.

"THE WORLD'S FASTEST"

THE WORLD'S FASTEST LONG DISTANCE RACE

Organised by THE BRITISH RACING DRIVERS' CLUB.

ADMISSION 3s. 6d. (including tax) CHILDREN 1s. 6d. (including tax)

DETAILS FROM

THE BRITISH RACING DRIVERS' CLUB, Ltd., Bangalore House, Newton Street, W.C.2 (Holborn 0161), or BROOKLANDS MOTOR COURSE, WEYBRIDGE, SURREY.

CHEAP COMBINED RAIL AND ADMISSION TICKETS FROM SOUTHERN RAILWAY STATIONS.

COVERED STANDS.

THE BOTOLPH PRINTING WORKS, CRANMER ROAD, BRIXTON ROAD, S.W.9

INTRODUCTION

TRAVELLING BY RAIL between Basingstoke and London, approaching Weybridge Station from the West, the traveller may notice the remains of a steeply banked concrete track, an impressive Edwardian building, a variety of sheds, and more curiously, several stranded aircraft parked miles from any runway. Surrounded by office buildings and supermarkets, this is all that remains today of Brooklands, a revolutionary purpose-built motor racing circuit and test track that dates from the earliest years of the motor car, and also a place that can claim to be the birthplace of much of the British aircraft industry.

Between 1907 and 1939 Brooklands was the acknowledged centre of motor sport in Britain for competitors on both two wheels and four, and a way of life for many enthusiasts. Not only was the Track a place where races were lost and won; speed records were set around the Outer Circuit, and the venue also welcomed the exciting new motor industry, which was able to test and prove its latest designs around the Outer Circuit and on the Test Hill.

The Clubhouse and Members' Hill also added a social dimension that attracted people from far and wide, giving summer weekends at the Weybridge venue a unique garden party atmosphere of tennis and tea dances.

However, Brooklands wasn't only the preserve of the sporting motorist and the pleasure seeker. Within the circuit an airfield was soon established, and spectators witnessed some great moments in the pioneering days of powered flight. Soon several flying schools were established, sending their students aloft in primitive contraptions that were the precursors of another revolution in transportation.

Before long an aircraft manufacturing industry grew up around the Track that would play a vital role in Britain's defence during two world wars, contributing many legendary aircraft to the war effort on both occasions, whilst between the wars the thriving Brooklands social scene also extended to the airfield as sports flying became ever more popular.

eventually the world of aviation took over the site completely – the last race meeting was held in 1939 – but Brooklands retains a place in the affections of many motor sport enthusiasts long after the final chequered flag was waved.

EARLY DAYS

DURING the Edwardian era, European motoring holidays were not for the faint-hearted. Mechanical unreliability, tyre problems, and thick clouds of dust were just some of the problems facing the intrepid motorist. Yet in 1905 wealthy Surrey landowners Hugh Locke King and his wife Ethel motored to Italy. They reached Brescia in time for the Coppa Florio road race and noticed that there were no British entrants. Discussing this with some of the competitors, Hugh was told that motoring was falling behind in Great Britain as restrictive laws prevented competition on the public roads and a British car would stand no chance against those from France and Italy.

Hugh was patriotic, and on his return to England he decided to see what he could do to improve the situation. He lived at Brooklands House just outside the Surrey town of Weybridge and had inherited a large estate with the ideal site for a permanent race track on some marshy ground cut by the River Wey, adjacent to the London & South Western railway line. That Weybridge Station was within easy walking distance was an added attraction, providing fast access to the future Track from central London. Although Hugh's patriotism is not in doubt, there was also a commercial motive behind the venture, as the Locke Kings saw the Track as a unique business opportunity.

Originally envisaged as a flat oval, costs increased dramatically when the designer, Colonel Holden of the Royal Engineers, suggested that the Track should have banked corners, which would allow speeds of up to 120 mph. Work proceeded on this basis – an enormous undertaking that relied on at least 1,500 labourers but was finished in just nine months. Using the latest construction methods, the Track was surfaced in concrete at least 6 inches thick and the River Wey was bridged using new concrete construction techniques pioneered by the Belgian Hennebique Company.

The man who started it all, Surrey landowner Hugh Locke King with his wife Ethel and a favourite poodle. A motoring holiday to Italy changed their lives forever.

Opposite: Percy Lambert and A. J. Hancock pioneered the streamlined single-seaters that set new standards at the Track prior to the First World War.

Blueprints for the Track, 1907. Constructing a purpose-built race track was a unique engineering project for the time, requiring fresh solutions and a vast army of labourers.

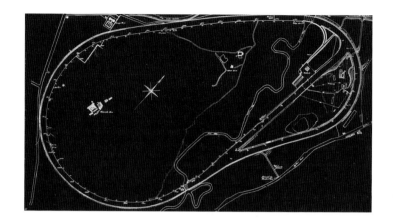

The construction of the Hennebique Bridge over the River Wey. The Belgian Hennebique Company pioneered the use of concrete for such structures.

When finished, the Track consisted of two great banked curves, known as the Home (or Members') Banking and the Byfleet Banking, joined on one side by the half-mile-long Railway Straight, and on the other by a gentler, unbanked reverse curve – rather than a straight – made necessary as Hugh had previously sold several parcels of land on this side of the Track.

A lap of the Outer Circuit measured 2.767 miles, with the Track 100 feet wide all around. About halfway along the reverse curve, the Finishing Straight ran from the Fork straight across to the Members' Banking, passing by the Paddock with its impressive Clubhouse. Opposite, on the Members' Hill between the Banking and the Finishing Straight, restaurants and seating were provided, with a bridge passing over the Members' Banking to provide access for the spectators.

The Clubhouse in 1907. It was modelled on the Mena House Hotel in Egypt, once owned by the Locke Kings. The centre of operations for the Track, it housed the Clerk of the Course's office.

A member of the family later claimed that the Track had cost Hugh around £150,000, a vast amount at the time, and the Locke Kings only remained solvent with the help of large mortgages and assistance from Ethel's family.

The Earl of Lonsdale opened the Track on Monday, 17 June 1907. Following lunch and a short speech from Hugh, a number of the guests followed the Locke Kings out onto the circuit for a parade lap, which rapidly became an impromptu race as the owners of the faster cars broke rank and began to enjoy the novel pleasure of unrestricted speed around the banked Track.

Menu for the opening lunch, June 1907. Hugh Locke King made a short speech, then he and his wife Ethel led the diners around the Track in the family Itala.

The Track was run by the Brooklands Automobile Racing Club (BARC) and managed by the Locke Kings' friend Count Rodakowski, a fiery autocrat with a reputation for getting things done. S. F. Edge, the winner of the 1902 Gordon Bennett Race and the sales agent for Napier cars, had already announced that he would make an attempt on the world 24 hours record with a team of three 60 hp Napiers, one driven solely by himself, as soon as the Track was completed. The attempt began on the evening of Friday, 28 June 1907, and during the night the drivers were forced to rely on red lanterns placed around the Track, with additional flares marking the top of the Banking. Despite this, Edge was triumphant, taking the record at an average speed of

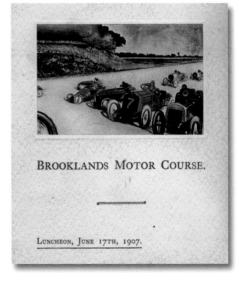

BROOKLANDS MOTOR COURSE.

LUNCHEON, JUNE 17TH, 1907.

9

The Finishing Straight and Clubhouse, just completed, in 1907. The sheer scale of Hugh Locke King's vision is apparent and the new motor course attracted incredulous visitors even before the official opening.

65.09 mph in front of a large crowd. Unfortunately there were unforeseen consequences as the freshly laid concrete had begun to break up and had to be patched with gravel, while the noise of three powerful cars circulating throughout the night also had long-term repercussions as the residents of Weybridge were not amused by the disturbance. Track degradation requiring annual wintertime repairs and complaints about noise were problems that would dog the Track for many years.

The first race meeting took place a week later but proved a disappointment. The crowd was much smaller than expected, whilst some of the rules, based closely on horse racing, failed to translate well to the new

S. F. Edge in the 24 Hours Record Napier, 1907. Although a great success for Edge and Napier, attracting fine publicity, the run caused problems for the Track in later years.

The vast expanse of the Banking could make some of the cars look slow, detracting from the spectacle in the early years.

motor racing arena. The cars weren't numbered, and the drivers wore the owner's colours, which made them difficult to distinguish at speed. The smaller-engined cars also seemed very slow on the vast expanse of concrete, and large differences in performance made some of the races less than exciting for the spectators.

Edwardian crowds on the Members' Hill shortly after the Track opened in 1907. Unfortunately attendance often fell below expectations in the early years.

Members' badge, 1907. The yellow and black colours were associated with Brooklands from the beginning. A sign in these colours on Weybridge Station directed passengers to the Track.

A composite image of the 1912 Rule Book, entrance tickets, mechanic's pass and BARC lapel badge.

The situation was greatly improved by Albert V. Ebblewhite (known to all as 'Ebby'), who introduced a system of handicapping using an electric timing system devised by Colonel Holden. By keeping meticulous records of every competitor, Ebby was able to produce close finishes between some widely varying machinery, although the more successful drivers tended to find themselves in a constant battle with the handicappers. Ebby also persuaded the BARC to let him number the cars and allow the press better access to the action. Bookmaking, however, was one horse racing tradition that remained throughout the life of the Track. Usually situated in the Paddock, and sometimes on the Members' Hill, bookmakers such as Jack Linton and Thomas 'Long Tom' Harris were a regular feature of Brooklands life, although the sums of money involved were generally low as the mechanical vagaries peculiar to motor sport made life difficult for punter and bookmaker alike.

From the earliest days, Locke King must have been gratified to see that the Track was used for testing and demonstrations by the motor trade. In 1908 the Royal Automobile Club's (RAC) 2,000 miles trial – run from London to Scotland and back – ended with a 200-mile high speed run around the Track. In the same year the English agent for the American Cadillac firm organised a unique demonstration. Three new single-cylinder Cadillacs were presented at the Track, did ten laps, then were completely stripped down. The components were jumbled up, then three cars were re-assembled from the pile of parts. Once rebuilt, the cars were driven around the track again in a stunt that emphasised quality of construction and interchangeability of components and earned the company the RAC's prestigious Dewar Trophy. S. F. Edge also enlivened the early years with a series of challenge races pitting his big Napiers against rivals from Mercedes and FIAT, in a series of contests that saw speeds rise dramatically, with Frank Newton's Napier 'Samson' being timed at 119 mph over half a mile in the autumn of 1908.

In 1909, Major Lindsay Lloyd replaced Rodakowski as Clerk of the Course and promptly made two decisions that altered the Brooklands scene forever. The most important was the creation of the airfield within the Track, whilst across the Finishing Straight from the Clubhouse a Test Hill was constructed, running up the side of the Members' Hill for 325 feet with an average gradient of 1:5, providing a useful test of both hill-climbing and braking efficiency.

Pure speed remained important. In November 1909, Victor Hemery brought the famous 200 hp 'Blitzen' Benz over from Germany and set a new world land speed record at 125.94 mph over a measured kilometre on the Railway Straight. Meanwhile at his works in Weybridge, Gordon Watney, a Weybridge motor trader, was pioneering the British race-tuning industry. Watney would buy second-hand Mercedes 60 hp and 90 hp limousines from the Mercedes importer, then strip them of their heavy coachwork and replace it with lightweight open bodywork constructed in aluminium by the Ewart Geyser Company. The engines were also tuned and the resulting machines proved both fast and reliable, winning numerous awards for their owners.

Major (later Colonel) Lindsay Lloyd, who inaugurated the Flying Village and the Test Hill as Clerk of the Course. A fine organiser, he remained at Brooklands until 1930.

During the Edwardian era few people could afford to commission such machines, but motorcycling was becoming popular amongst younger sportsmen. In February 1908 two Oxford undergraduates held a match race at the Track with the approval of the BARC. W. Gordon McMinnies, riding a Triumph, and Oscar Bickford, on a Vindec Special, raced over one lap, with McMinnies winning at 53.55 mph. Rodakowski was impressed, and invited several leading motorcyclists to a race during the Easter Monday meeting, when Will Cook on an NLG-Peugeot won at 63 mph and received a prize of 25 guineas for his efforts.

A second race in May introduced handicapping for the two-wheeled brigade and later in the year Charlie Collier took to the Track to break the world one-hour record on his JAP vee-twin-engined Matchless. Both Charlie and Harry Collier became star performers, riding for the family-owned Matchless brand, proving their machinery in speed events at Brooklands and on the Isle of Man.

In 1909 the British Motor Cycle Racing Club (BMCRC) was formed and in May held a one hour race, won by Harry Bashall. Long-distance races were to become a regular feature at BMCRC (usually pronounced 'Bemsee') meetings as well as the usual short handicaps. The motorcycle meetings tended to attract a smaller, more knowledgeable crowd, interested in the

Charlie and Harry Collier were successful performers at the Track before the First World War on their Matchless-JAPs. The brothers also competed successfully in the Isle of Man Tourist Trophy races.

technical details and keen on the longer events that demonstrated the reliability of the machinery.

In 1910 American-made Indian machines took the first three places in the one hour race, with second place going to Walter Owen Bentley, later famous as the designer of the Bentley motorcar. The following year Charlie Collier went head to head with the American champion Jake de Rosier – Matchless versus Indian – for a series of three two-lap races around the Track. De Rosier won the challenge in the third race but Collier responded in August, breaking the American's speed record with a run of 91.31 mph over a mile.

Meanwhile the more progressive car manufacturers were looking ahead, developing slender single-seaters that were capable of high lap speeds despite having smaller engines. The first was the Vauxhall KN that appeared in 1909, driven by A. J. Hancock. It was based on Laurence Pomeroy's advanced 20 hp design, with a monobloc four-cylinder engine of just over 3 litres' capacity, fitted with a long radiator cowl and slender wind-cheating bodywork just wide enough for the driver.

The KN set a trend followed by other progressive manufacturers and in early 1913 Percy Lambert drove his single-seater Talbot to a new world one-hour record, at an average speed of 103.8 mph. This feat caught the public's imagination, making Lambert one of the Track's first stars, and later in the year the French ace, Jules Goux, brought over a Peugeot Grand Prix car in an attempt to eclipse Lambert's time. The Peugeot, with several litres' advantage over Lambert's Talbot, eventually pushed the record up to 106.22 mph, but Goux did not hold the record for long.

In August Louis Coatalen of Sunbeam harnessed a 9-litre V12 Mohawk aero-engine into a single-seater for use on the Track. The big problem was tyre wear. Despite the Sunbeam having an engine twice the size of Lambert's Talbot, and a far higher top speed, for the hour-long run it was held down to around 110 mph to preserve the tyres as the French driver Jean Chassagne eased the record up to 107.95 mph.

Tyre problems also held back the big 'Blitzen' Benz driven by Ligurd G. 'Cupid' Hornsted. The car was a development of Hemery's record-breaking machine and its potential was not in doubt – Hornsted set a new world record of 124.09 mph over a mile at the Track – but although Hornsted had his eye on the one-hour record the tyres would always prove his undoing. Sadly the same was also true of Percy Lambert, who became the Track's first high-profile casualty in October when his Talbot overturned, killing the driver, during an attempt to regain the record.

Racing continued in 1914, but as the summer approached the international situation cast a shadow over the Track. Shortly after the August Bank Holiday meeting, Great Britain declared war on Germany and normal motoring activity ceased for the duration as the Royal Flying Corps (RFC) took over the site.

All racing effectively ended on the outbreak of war, but two sprint meetings were held for services personnel in 1915. The uniforms with white lapels denote the wearers as injured soldiers housed in local hospitals. Although these meetings must have been successful morale boosters, they were soon discontinued.

INTO THE AIR

From the beginning, enthusiasts for the new science of powered flight had recognised that Brooklands was an ideal venue for further experimentation and the BARC announced an award of £2,500 to the first aviator to complete a full circuit of the Track during 1907. At the time nobody had succeeded in making even a brief hop in Britain, but Alliot Verdon Roe arrived at Brooklands and persuaded a sceptical Rodakowski to allow him to house his aeroplane – built in a Putney garage – in a purpose-build shed alongside the Finishing Straight.

Roe was both short of funds and unlucky. His early experiments were hampered by an inadequate 6 hp JAP engine and he probably never made a sustained flight, even with a loaned 24 hp Antoinette engine. But Roe persevered, building an improved triplane that he promptly crashed. This was too much for Rodakowski and he gave Roe notice to quit. The pioneer moved to Manchester where he developed a new triplane, but changes at the Track soon permitted his return.

In 1909 Rodakowski was replaced as Clerk of the Course by Lindsay Lloyd, whilst Louis Bleriot's achievement in flying across the English Channel aroused greater interest in powered flight in Britain. George Holt Thomas, a newspaper proprietor and entrepreneur, organised a demonstration in Blackpool by the French aviator Louis Paulham. This was a great success and Holt Thomas persuaded the Brooklands authorities to repeat the show. At the end of October 1909 Paulham gave an impressive display with a Henri Farman biplane, making several short flights, then taking both his wife and the intrepid Ethel Locke King as passengers in turn. He also made a flight of over 90 miles, the longest recorded so far in Great Britain.

The enthusiastic response to this demonstration resulted in the establishment of the Flying Village at the Byfleet end of the Track, where Lloyd supervised the erection of several sheds on the inside of the Byfleet Banking. These were available at a rent of £100 per annum, or £10 per month, payable in advance. The sheds were soon taken up and aviation became a permanent part of the Brooklands scene. Two of the earliest inhabitants were Helmuth

Opposite:
As the crowd lines the top of the banking, a pioneer aviator puts on a display at an early flying meeting. These attracted greater crowds than the motor racing meetings held before the First World War. (IWM RAE-O 798)

A.V. Roe with his aircraft in the shed built to house it alongside the Finishing Straight. He was so short of money that he often slept in the shed.

The first flying sheds, with Thomas Sopwith well to the fore. This was the beginnings of a great aircraft manufacturing concern that would prove invaluable to the country in two world wars.

Martin and George Handasyde, who would later produce Martinsyde aeroplanes, while Roe returned to Brooklands with two triplanes and immediately impressed onlookers with their fine performance and stability.

One of the sheds was converted into the Blue Bird Restaurant by Mr and Mrs Eardley Billing. This soon became the social centre for the flying colony as more and more enthusiasts began to gravitate towards the airfield. Instruction was catered for by several flying schools, one of the first being opened by the French pilot Gustav Blondeau, in partnership with Hilda Hewlett, the first woman to qualify as a pilot in Britain. Besides instruction, several of the schools also offered flights to the public and this became so

/rewrt

popular that in 1911 Keith Prowse, the London ticket agency, opened a booking office on the airfield.

In October 1910 a yachtsman called Thomas Sopwith arrived at Brooklands, intent on learning to fly. He was a fast learner and by late November he had set a British duration record of 107.75 miles in 3 hours, 12 minutes and 55 seconds flying a 60 hp Howard Wright biplane. Sopwith began to take part in flying competitions but would soon turn his hobby into a business.

By 1911, air racing was becoming popular. In May Gustav Hamel, flying a Bleriot monoplane, won a race from Brooklands to Brighton. Shortly afterwards the Daily Mail sponsored the first Round Britain Air Race with a first prize of £10,000. The event caught the public's imagination and a huge crowd gathered to watch the aircraft depart. Starting from Brooklands, the competitors made a short hop to Hendon, then headed north as far as Stirling. Turning south, they visited Carlisle, Manchester and Bristol, then touched the south coast at Brighton before finally returning to Brooklands. The winner was André Beaumont in a Bleriot, ahead of fellow Frenchman Jules Védrines, after 22 hours of flying spread over five days.

The Blue Bird Restaurant c.1912. This soon became the social centre for anyone involved in flying at Brooklands before the First World War. The small cubicle in front is the flight ticket office.

Keith Prowse, the London ticket agency, began booking flights in 1911. Despite the primitive aircraft available, there was no shortage of intrepid passengers willing to sample powered flight.

André Beaumont arriving back at Brooklands in his Bleriot to win the Daily Mail Round Britain Race in 1911. The next day he was presented to King George V at Buckingham Palace.

An advertisement for Hewlett & Blondeau, one of the first flying schools established at Brooklands, which also manufactured Farman aircraft and offered flights to the public.

By the following year the military had woken up to the potential of aviation and the Royal Flying Corps was formed. As prospective pilots were to receive basic training at civilian flying schools, this was another boost for the Brooklands schools. Later in the year Thomas Sopwith decided to move into manufacturing after carrying out some successful conversion work on existing aircraft in his sheds. Sopwith had a knack for choosing the right associates, with the Australian Harry Hawker as test pilot, and Fred Sigrist overseeing the engineering. The new company converted an old skating rink at Kingston-upon-Thames into a factory, but retained its premises at Brooklands, where final assembly and testing took place.

Meanwhile Roe had received several orders for his latest Type 500 biplane. Its successor, the Type 504, was produced at his Manchester factory, but flew first at Brooklands in 1913. The Type 504 became famous as one of the finest training aircraft of the next twenty years and many were flown from the Brooklands airfield. In the same year Sopwith produced the Tabloid, a small, relatively fast aircraft aimed at the military market, which was now expanding as a major European war looked increasingly likely. The Tabloid was first flown and developed at Brooklands. Fitted with floats, one was taken to Monte Carlo where it won the Schneider Trophy in April 1914, flown by Howard Pixton, who had learnt his trade at Brooklands under Roe.

In August 1914 Great Britain declared war on Germany and Hugh Locke King immediately made Brooklands available to the government. The fledgling RFC moved in and the flying schools were taken over

HEWLETT & BLONDEAU

Licensed Farman Biplane
— (BUILT AT BROOKLANDS) —
came in 16 minutes before
ANY OTHER Biplane in the
Brooklands to Brighton Race.

Piloted by LIEUTENANT SNOWDEN-SMITH.

and adapted to military requirements. Besides flight training, the airfield was also used for the testing of new aircraft, and the formation of new squadrons, and a wireless and observer school was established. The Blue Bird Restaurant became the officers' mess, but burnt down in 1917 during a fire that also damaged several of the adjacent hangars.

In March 1915 Vickers Limited, the armaments manufacturer, took over the Itala works adjacent to the Fork and began to expand the facility, completing the purchase later in the year. The company already had a Brooklands presence, with a flying school closely linked to the RFC, as well as using the airfield for testing. Now, as well as producing its own designs, including the Vickers Gunbus – the first purpose-built fighter aircraft – Vickers also began to mass-produce aircraft designed at the Royal Aircraft Factory at Farnborough, including the BE2c reconnaissance aircraft

A programme for the Daily Mail Round Britain Race. The event caught the public imagination and the start attracted enormous crowds of spectators to the Track.

Thomas Sopwith flying his Howard Wright monoplane with the Track in the background. Sopwith was a natural aviator who set distance records within months of gaining his licence.

An SE5a, recently completed, at the Vickers works, c. 1917. Designed at the Royal Aircraft Factory at Farnborough, the aircraft was one of the finest produced in the First World War.

During the First World War, women had a vital role to play in aircraft production, the manufacture of munitions and agricultural work; the beginnings of a social revolution. This happy scene celebrates the completion of the 1000th SE5a.

and the FE8. During 1917 the factory began to turn out the Royal Aircraft Factory's SE5a scout, one of the best British fighters of the war, ultimately producing 2,165, whilst Martinsyde produced a further 500 examples at Brooklands.

Thomas Sopwith had expanded his factory at Kingston but still continued to carry out the final erection and testing of aircraft such as the Sopwith Pup and the Camel at Brooklands, where Harry Hawker occasionally enlivened test sessions by flying underneath the footbridge crossing the Byfleet Banking. As the war drew to a close, Sopwith introduced the Snipe, a fighter that would remain

in service with the new Royal Air Force (RAF) until well into the 1920s.

Meanwhile, Vickers was working on a design for a long-distance bomber capable of reaching into the heart of Germany. The Rex Pierson-designed Vickers Vimy arrived too late to influence the outcome of the war, but gained everlasting fame in 1919 when John Alcock and Arthur Whitten-Brown succeeded in crossing the Atlantic Ocean between Newfoundland and Ireland. The following year another Vimy, flown by Ross and Keith Smith of the Royal Australian Air Force, became the first aircraft to fly from England to Australia.

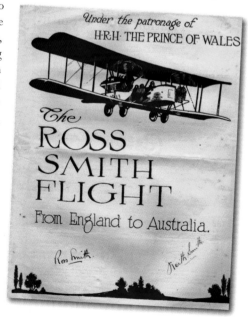

A Vickers Vimy under construction. Although the aircraft arrived too late to make a difference to the First World War, it found fame with several record-breaking flights.

A souvenir of the Ross and Keith Smith flight to Australia, signed by the two brothers. The Smith brothers were knighted for their exploits and their aircraft remains on display in Adelaide.

BACK ON TRACK

A LTHOUGH the war ended in November 1918, enthusiasts hoping to see some racing in 1919 were to be disappointed. The Track had been badly damaged by the RFC's (later the RAF's) lorries and substantial repairs were necessary. Racing was finally set to resume on Easter Monday in April 1920, but heavy rain caused the meeting to be postponed. A large crowd had turned up, eager to see some action after such a long break, and, not wishing to disappoint them, Malcolm Campbell – later to become famous as the holder of the world land speed record – put on a couple of impromptu match races, winning both. The postponed meeting was run the following Saturday and Campbell won once again in his 1912 Lorraine-Dietrich Grand Prix car, the first race winner at Brooklands following the war.

In June, Louis Coatalen produced his latest development on the aero-engined theme when Harry Hawker exchanged his usual aeroplane cockpit for four wheels and introduced the new 18.3-litre V12 Sunbeam. Unfortunately a tyre burst during testing and the car smashed through the fencing along the Railway Straight. Hawker was unhurt, but the big Sunbeam's debut was delayed. By 1922 the car was a race winner, and in May Kenelm Lee Guinness demonstrated its potential by setting a new world land speed record at 133.75 mph over a measured kilometre along the Railway Straight, the last occasion that the record would be set at Brooklands.

June 1920 also marked the debut of the flamboyant Count Louis Zborowski at Brooklands, driving a 1914 Grand Prix Mercedes. In August he took his first win at the Track and the following year he produced his legendary aero-engined creation, 'Chitty-Bang-Bang', a pre-war Mercedes chassis fitted with a 23-litre Maybach engine from a Gotha bomber. This large and spectacular machine, the first of a series, delighted the fans and always attracted a lot of attention in the Brooklands Paddock until the count's death during the 1924 Italian Grand Prix at Monza. Other drivers, including the Wolseley company's racing manager Sir Alastair Miller, produced similar concoctions. Miller fitted a large V8 Hispano–Suiza aero-engine (built under license by Wolseley) into an old Napier chassis, apparently sourced from the

Opposite:
As Brooklands became established on the social calendar, the Paddock became a popular showcase for all the latest ladies' fashions.

royal estate at Sandringham! The resulting machine, known as 'The Viper', eventually lapped the Track at over 110 mph, but in the meantime other competitors were taking a more scientific approach to speed.

In 1922 John Godfrey Parry Thomas made his first race appearance at the Track driving a stripped 7-litre Leyland Eight. It was not an auspicious debut – the Leyland stripped its clutch at the start – but the Welshman was destined to become perhaps the greatest Outer Circuit ace of all. Thomas was the chief engineer at Leyland Motors and had designed the impressive Leyland Eight to challenge Rolls-Royce at the pinnacle of the luxury market. He somehow managed to persuade the Leyland directors to allow him to race one at the Track in standard form, but the Brooklands magic gripped Thomas straight away and he soon began to modify the car in the search for more speed. Parting company with Leyland, in 1923 he moved into a bungalow known as 'The Hermitage' in the Flying Village. He worked through a series of modifications that resulted in the streamlined Leyland Thomas, which took him to many race wins, as well as setting a lap record of 129.36 mph in 1925. His match race over ten laps the same year, for stakes of £500, against Ernest Eldridge in the 21.7-litre aero-engined FIAT 'Mephistopheles' produced a stunning display of high-speed motoring, with both cars losing tyre treads before Thomas swept by the FIAT on the last lap to win at 123.23 mph.

A.V. (Ebby) Ebblewhite starting a typical handicap event in 1927. Three Bugattis can be seen in the line-up. Ebby's contribution to the Track, as starter and handicapper, ensured its success after a shaky start.

The BARC season usually began in March or April and ran through until September, with meetings taking place on the usual Bank Holidays at Easter, Whitsun and August, with a final meeting in September or October. The club tended to run several short sharp handicap races at each meeting – the short handicaps over one flying lap, the long handicaps over two – with a longer race of 25, 50, or 100 miles as the main event. Most races were run on handicap and provided plenty of action on track, whilst the Clubhouse provided a different type of entertainment after the last race of the day. By the late 1920s Brooklands had become a popular fixture on the social scene alongside Henley, Wimbledon and Ascot, as society attempted to forget the privations and sacrifice of the recent war. Although it was originally hoped for as many as 30,000 spectators at race meetings, in practice the numbers were usually much smaller, although the BARC made a virtue of this by advertising that Brooklands attracted 'The right crowd... and no crowding'!

Other clubs, such as the Junior Car Club (JCC) and the Surbiton Motor Club, held similar meetings, and often proved more adventurous than the BARC. During the 1920s the motoring

The infamous match race between Ernest Eldridge in the FIAT Mephistopheles and J. G. Parry Thomas in the Leyland-Thomas. Thomas overtook Eldridge to win on the last lap, despite both cars losing tyre treads during the race.

The Junior Car Club 200 miles race was the country's premier race meeting in the early 1920s and received plenty of attention in the motoring press. The advanced Anglo-French Talbot Darracqs usually dominated the race.

scene was expanding rapidly, with a greater emphasis on smaller, less expensive cars, and in 1921 the JCC announced a 200 miles race for light cars up to 1,500cc, which proved the most important race of the year. Amongst the entry were three purpose-built Talbot Darracqs – miniature Grand Prix cars from the Anglo-French Sunbeam-Talbot-Darracq concern – which dominated the '200', setting new standards for small car performance until 1923 when Major Harvey scored a popular home victory in an Alvis.

In the 1920s, motorcyclists had to be tough. The BMCRC had ambitious plans for longer races, and in July 1921 it held a 500 miles race that developed into a duel between Bert Le Vack's Indian and the Harley-Davidsons ridden by Douglas Davidson and Freddie Dixon. Tyres always played an important part in long-distance races on the Outer Circuit, and Le Vack lost an early lead with a puncture. Davidson and Dixon took over, only for Dixon to have a blow-out on the Railway Straight that threw him from the machine. He recovered to finish second to Le Vack by 10 minutes, but Davidson wasn't so lucky. Plagued by a wartime injury and struggling with mechanical problems, he accepted help to push his machine back to the pits and was duly disqualified for receiving outside assistance. The 500 miles race was never repeated, but in June 1922 the Ealing and District Club ran a 200 miles race for sidecar combinations, and Davidson, now riding an Indian, had the satisfaction of leading home Le Vack on a Zenith-JAP.

Motorcycle competitors assembling at the Fork before the start. Despite appearances, the starting process was well organised as usual by Mr Ebblewhite.

Bert Denly on the Norton-Hughes motorcycle and sidecar outfit he used to win the 1928 200 miles race. It was later used by Pat Driscoll with great success for racing and record-breaking.

Motorcycle speeds were rising all the time. In late October 1922 Le Vack defied a damp track to cover 5 miles at 100.29 mph, despite intermittent drizzle, recording the first Outer Circuit lap at over 100 mph on two wheels. The following month he set a new hour record at 89.86 mph on his 980cc Zenith-JAP.

In 1923 the BMCRC ran two 200 miles races on the same day. Once again the event was a triumph for Le Vack, who won the 350/250cc race in the morning on a New Imperial-JAP, then took to a 996cc Brough Superior for the second race, winning that as well. The 500cc class was won by a new star, Bert Denly, riding a Norton. Only months before, Denly had been a butcher's delivery boy riding a pre-war motorcycle. Legend relates that one day he narrowly avoided a collision with the ace Norton tuner Daniel R. 'Don' O'Donovan. Realising that the youngster was a born rider, O'Donovan persuaded Denly to take up track riding and he proved so good that he soon set a new 500cc hour record at 82.66 mph, then won the 500cc class in the '200', his first big race at the Track!

Occasionally the longer races proved too hard on the machinery. In the 1926 200 miles sidecar races, only one machine finished the 600cc race, when Victor Horsman had a lonely ride across the finish line on his Triumph outfit. It was a quiet finish too, as he coasted over the line with a dead engine. The manufacturers hardly craved that type of publicity, and as several Nortons had retired during the race, a few days later the management had Denly and fellow works rider Pat Driscoll out taking long-distance records in an effort to remedy the adverse headlines.

In 1926 the BMCRC, coinciding with the Motor Cycle Show at Olympia, held a series of Grand Prix motorcycle races at the Track. Instead of using the Outer Circuit, a much shorter course was devised. Starting on the Finishing Straight by the Clubhouse, the riders turned right onto the Members' Banking then ran down to the Fork, where they took a sharp right hairpin-turn back onto the Finishing Straight, negotiating an artificial bend just before the Start/Finish line. This course became known as the Mountain Circuit, and it provided plenty of action until the close of the Track in 1939. At the first meeting, the winner of the 250cc race was Eric Fernihough, who would become one of the motorcycling world's biggest stars. Another great Brooklands character was E. C. E. 'Barry' Baragwanath, who had made his mark aboard a big Brough Superior combination. Baragwanath was a large man who always wore a winged collar, even when racing. He won the 1,000cc Sidecar Championship in 1926 and again in 1928, having also won the 200 miles sidecar race in 1927. Always ready to help other competitors, Baragwanath finally retired from racing at the age

Noel Pope
at speed on a
Norton. Pope set
the ultimate Outer
Circuit lap record
at 124.51 mph on
two wheels with
the ex-Baragwanath
supercharged
Brough Superior
just weeks before
the Track closed
for good in 1939.

of 50 having lapped the Outer Circuit at over 100 mph on numerous occasions. His supercharged Brough passed to Noel Pope, who improved the machine further. Running it without a sidecar, Pope finally set the all-time two-wheeled Outer Circuit record at 124.51 mph in July 1939, only weeks before the Track closed forever.

Enthusiasts watch
the 1933 New
Zealand Trophy
race get underway.
The motorcycle
races usually
started opposite
the Vickers factory
by the Fork.

The high speed trials organised by both the Motor Cycle Club and the Junior Car Club always attracted plenty of entrants and gave many drivers their first experience of the Track.

During the week Brooklands was always busy, with racing machinery being tested and new vehicles on trial – even double-decker buses climbing the Test Hill. The motoring press used the Track to test new cars and motorcycles, and for a few shillings anybody could join in the fun and lap the Outer Circuit in their own car or motorcycle. But not everyone visited Brooklands to take part in adventures on the Track. During summer weekends, Brooklands regularly took on a garden party atmosphere. With no racing on Sundays, entry to the Paddock was free and the restaurants on the Members' Hill were kept busy with regular tea dances while the tennis courts were also available to visitors.

Realising that not every enthusiast wanted to race, but that many might enjoy some time on the Track, the JCC announced its first high speed trial in 1925. This was run over a circuit that combined the Finishing Straight and the Byfleet Banking with the Track's service roads – closed to normal traffic for the length of the trial – that took the competitors outside the Members' Banking, bringing them back onto the Finishing Straight via the Members' Bridge and down the Test Hill. The event was run against the clock and different average speeds were set for the three classes (up to 1,100cc, 1,100 to 1,500cc, and sports cars up to 1,500cc). The event was not a race, but those that bettered their set speeds received the Club's Gold Award.

The trial proved a spectacular success, attracting both novice and professional alike. Amongst many others, the competitors included *The Autocar's* sports editor, S. C. H. 'Sammy' Davis, and a young Alec Issigonis, who years later would design the Morris Minor and the Mini, driving his mother's Singer Ten.

The success of the JCC's high speed trial encouraged the Motor Cycle Club (MCC) to run its own event for cars later in the year. This was restricted to the Outer Circuit and was a flat-out blast over 37 laps. This soon showed up any weaknesses, with broken valves and failed big-ends halting several cars in the early laps. The target speeds were relatively low, however, 37 mph for cars up to 1,100cc, 40 mph for cars up to 1,500cc and 45 mph for the fastest cars, resulting in virtually everybody who finished winning a Gold Award. Once again the event proved a great success, and the MCC repeated the event annually along with similar runs for the motorcyclists. For the more adventurous, the popular magazine *The Motor Cycle* held its Clubman's Days; a mixture of races and sprints at the start of the season, when hundreds of amateur riders enjoyed a taste of competition on the Track.

In 1926 Grand Prix racing arrived in Surrey when the RAC announced that Brooklands would host the first British Grand Prix. The race was to run anticlockwise, using the Finishing Straight, the Railway Straight and the Byfleet Banking, with chicanes placed on the Finishing Straight in an attempt to mimic a road circuit. Unfortunately the race was not a success.

The Junior Car Club high speed trial incorporated the Test Hill in the route as well as the Track's service roads to provide an interesting mixed route that also incorporated much of the Outer Circuit.

Apart from his record-breaking exploits, Malcolm Campbell had many successes at the Track in cars like this Bugatti T35. He finished second in a Bugatti in the first British Grand Prix in 1926.

Only nine cars took part and the event was mostly memorable for the dominant Delage team almost defeating themselves with a poorly designed exhaust system that roasted the driver's feet! Eventually, after numerous driver changes, the team managed to get a car home in first place in front of Malcolm Campbell in his Bugatti. The Grand Prix returned in 1927 but was even less exciting than the previous year. Robert Benoist dominated the race in his Delage in the absence of any serious competition, and the event never returned to Brooklands.

One car that didn't make the start in 1926 was Parry Thomas's revolutionary new, low-built 1.5-litre car, popularly known as the 'Flatiron'. By October, Thomas had the new car running well and drove one to victory in a 50 miles handicap race in front of the king of Iraq, but it was a farewell performance by the Welsh ace. The following spring he was killed at Pendine Sands, attempting to regain the land speed record in 'Babs', his Liberty aero-engined car developed from one of Count Zborowski's projects.

By the mid-1920s the British success in the 24 Hours Race at Le Mans was generating enormous interest in long-distance sports car racing, especially since a Bentley had won the race in 1924. Correspondence in *The Autocar* suggested that something similar should be held in this country, and

For many years Malcolm Campbell had a permanent presence at Brooklands. Here a schoolboy watches a Mercedes 38/250 being prepared outside Campbell's shed.

the magazine gave Sammy Davis the task of finding a club to organise a suitable event. The Essex Motor Club rose to the challenge, holding a 6 hours race at Brooklands in May 1927. The cars were close to standard specification and those over 1,500cc had to have four seats. Depending on engine size, each class of car had a set distance to surpass, and *The Autocar* provided a cup for the car that beat its handicap by the widest margin. The Bentley patron Woolf Barnato also provided a cup for the car that travelled the greatest distance outright.

The circuit ran along the Finishing Straight around two sand bank chicanes, then turned left onto the Railway Straight and proceeded around the Byfleet Banking to rejoin the Finishing Straight at the Fork. The entry was strong, with teams from the leading British sporting manufacturers, Bentley, Alvis, Sunbeam, and Lea Francis amongst others, and the race proved a great success, with Sammy Davis, driving an Alvis, winning his own magazine's cup. Meanwhile, Barnato managed to force a smile as he saw his cup go to a Sunbeam driven by George Duller.

The following year Fred Styles, the Alfa Romeo importer, realised that the race was a fine opportunity to showcase the performance of the advanced new six-cylinder Alfa Romeos with their small, but supercharged, 1,500cc engines. Giulio Ramponi, a factory test driver, was loaned by the factory in Milan and duly obliged by winning the race. In 1929 Woolf Barnato decided to attend to business himself, winning for Bentley with Jack Dunfee, but in the meantime the ever-inventive JCC had come up with an idea to rival the popular 24 Hours Race at Le Mans, the Double-12 Hours Race.

Racing at night had been impossible at Brooklands since Edge's 24 hours run back in 1907, so the JCC decided to run the race in two 12-hour heats, the cars being kept in parc ferme – a neutral zone, where no work on cars was permitted – overnight. In 1929 Giulio Ramponi returned to the Track to win the race for Alfa Romeo, driving the whole distance single-handed, with Sammy Davis and Sir Roland Gunter finishing second for Bentley. The following May, Sammy finished second once again as Woolf Barnato and Frank Clement took the top honours in a Bentley Speed Six, but in 1931 the MG team from Abingdon confounded the handicappers, taking a surprise victory with the tiny, supercharged C-type MG.

The following year the JCC replaced the event with a 1,000 miles race, again split over two days. It resulted in an historic victory for Elsie Wisdom and Joan Richmond in a Riley, averaging 81.41 mph. Unfortunately, interest in this type of racing was now waning and attendance figures were poor, so this was to be the last of the long-distance sports car races held at the Track.

1932 race card. The rear cover carries an advertisement for *The Motor* magazine. Both it and *The Autocar* regularly covered racing at Brooklands.

35

CIVIL
AIR DISPLAY

BROOKLANDS
MAY 28th.

ADMISSION 2/6 & 5/-. CARS 2/6

FLYING BETWEEN THE WARS

THE 1918 Armistice meant the end of large government orders for the aircraft industry, and the cutbacks in production had dire results for the manufacturers operating from the airfield. Martinsyde didn't survive, whilst Thomas Sopwith's company went into voluntary receivership when faced with a huge bill for back-tax on their wartime profits. However Sopwith would soon return to the business with a new venture, the H. G. Hawker Engineering Company – named after Sopwith's old friend Harry Hawker – based at the old Kingston factory.

Post-war, the flying school tradition was revived by Lieutenant-Colonel George Henderson with two Avro 504 trainers based in sheds opposite the Byfleet Banking. By 1928 Henderson had tired of the business and sold out to his chief instructor, Duncan Davis, who renamed the business the Brooklands School of Flying. The new owner had no money but a passion for flying, having run away from school to help the pioneer Colonel Cody with his early aircraft. During the First World War, Davis joined the RFC as a mechanic, then gained his wings and served with distinction on the Western Front. Times were hard at first, but Davis was able to count on support from several wealthy clients as well as members of his family, and by 1929 he had eight aircraft in use.

Meanwhile the De Havilland company was producing the Moth range, a series of low-priced, reliable, light aircraft. These, and similar aircraft such as the Avro Avian, introduced private aviation to a new market and guaranteed a steady supply of pupils for the flying school.

In early 1930 the Brooklands Aero Club (BAC) was formed by the BARC, one of the first members being HRH Prince George, later Duke of Kent. The new club had excellent relations with the flying school and thrived, building a new Clubhouse, complete with control tower, in 1932. This was an ultra-modern concrete structure designed by Graham Dawbarn, with a restaurant, lounges, showers and offices, which set new standards. Meanwhile the flying school moved into a large new hangar directly behind the new building.

Opposite: During the twenties, flying continued to intrigue the general public, and regular displays at Brooklands competed for attention with the motor racing scene. Eventually aviation would take over the site completely.

Davis's business sense served Brooklands well. He promoted weekend flying meetings and social events and encouraged London business people to arrange lunchtime flying lessons, relying on the fast rail connection between Waterloo Station and Weybridge. The flying school also developed a scheme with *The Tatler*, whereby fifty people were given free trials during the year, the best five pupils receiving free instruction to the basic 'A' licence standard.

Throughout the 1930s Brooklands hosted numerous air shows and flying days, providing a fascinating mixture of private flying, new commercial developments and the latest military aircraft.

On the social side, Davis (known as 'The Skipper') invented the idea of dawn patrols in partnership with affiliated clubs. These required visiting pilots to evade the home club 'defenders' and land before being spotted, thus winning a free breakfast in the Clubhouse. The BAC was always generous regarding landing fees, and Thomson and Taylor, with their workshops close at hand, were well qualified to overhaul light aircraft engines, so that private flying prospered at the Track throughout the 1930s.

Emphasising that Brooklands was now firmly back in the forefront of private aviation, the big air races returned to the Weybridge airfield. In 1932 the King's Cup Air Race was based at Brooklands. Won by Walter Hope flying a De Havilland Fox Moth, the second aircraft home was a Comper Swift entered by the Prince of Wales and flown by his personal pilot, Flight Lieutenant Edward Fielden. Brooklands was also the starting point for the London to Newcastle race the same year, when Fielden set the fastest time in the prince's Comper Swift.

Unfortunately, during the 1930s the international situation became ever more menacing and Davis began to advertise flying lessons as

Following a 'dawn patrol', a group photograph in front of the new Clubhouse with the School of Flying hangar visible in the background. Duncan Davis, 'The Skipper', is standing to the left of the lady in the centre.

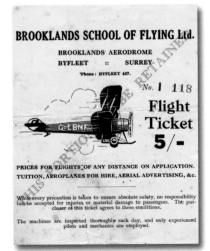

BROOKLANDS SCHOOL OF FLYING Ltd.

BROOKLANDS AERODROME
BYFLEET :: SURREY
'Phone: BYFLEET 437.

No. I 118

Flight
Ticket
5/-

PRICES FOR FLIGHTS OF ANY DISTANCE ON APPLICATION.
TUITION, AEROPLANES FOR HIRE, AERIAL ADVERTISING, &c.

While every precaution is taken to ensure absolute safety, no responsibility can be accepted for injuries or material damage to passengers. The purchaser of this ticket agrees to these conditions.

The machines are inspected thoroughly each day, and only experienced pilots and mechanics are employed.

The Brooklands School of Flying maintained the pre-First World War tradition by offering the flights to the public at reasonable prices.

'A Duty and a Pleasure'. Meanwhile the Vickers and Hawker factories began to increase production of military aircraft in response to the growing threat from Nazi Germany. During the 1920s and early 1930s Vickers had produced a fine series of bombers and transport aircraft including the Virginia and Victoria, while Hawker had concentrated on smaller single-engined machines, in particular the outstanding Hart series of light bomber and fighter aircraft. This experience would stand both companies in good stead as they introduced two outstanding new designs when the country rearmed to face the threat from Nazi Germany.

The King's Cup Air Race returned to Brooklands in the 1930s. The sport thrived throughout the decade and helped to maintain Brooklands' position at the centre of private aviation in Britain.

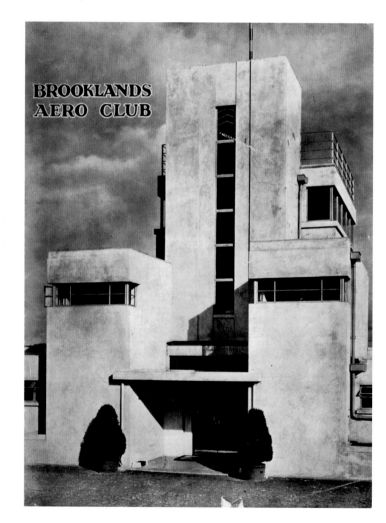

Brave New World! The Brooklands Aero Club opened its new Clubhouse in May 1932, the same year that Aldous Huxley's famous novel was published. The new Clubhouse quickly became the centre for social events at the Track.

BROOKLANDS AT HOME

JUNE 1st, 1935.

ADMIT BEARER TO AERODROME

(Please display this badge prominently).

Left: The Brooklands At Home meetings proved very popular in the 1930s. Large crowds attended these air shows where the manufacturers would often display their latest designs, flown by their top test pilots.

Below: Brooklands Aviation Limited was responsible for running the airfield and the flying school. The directors included Percy Bradley, who was also the Clerk of the Course for the BARC, and Duncan Davis.

BROOKLANDS
(WEYBRIDGE)
THE BRITISH
1000 MILES
RACE
FRI. & SAT.
JUNE 3 & 4
Gordon Crosby
ORGANISED BY THE JUNIOR CAR CLUB
RACING 10 A.M. to 5·30 P.M. EACH DAY
CHEAP COMBINED RAIL & ADMISSION TICKETS TO WEYBRIDGE FROM S.R. STATIONS

SERIOUS SPEED

IN 1929 the British Racing Drivers Club (BRDC) decided to host a race for pure racing cars over 500 miles on the Outer Circuit, unencumbered by chicanes or other obstacles. Considering the high speeds envisaged and the state of the ageing Track, they decided to hold the event in October to allow entrants time to rebuild their cars for the following season. Sammy Davis was on hand to report the race for *The Autocar*, but was coerced into driving a big 6½-litre Bentley that was considered too difficult around the Outer Circuit by the regular drivers. As usual the event was handicapped, with five classes ranging from up to 1,100cc to over 5 litres, the fastest cars starting at least 2 hours after the smallest. Five of the big Bentleys, and a handful of Grand Prix cars from Sunbeam, Bugatti, and Alfa Romeo headed the field.

The competitors assembled on the Finishing Straight and were started according to their class at the Fork – so after the first group started this meant that the next class was marshalled on the Track while the earlier starters raced past. Twenty-eight cars took the start and the winners of the first BRDC '500' were Frank Clement and Jack Barclay in a 4½-litre Bentley, followed home by Davis and Clive Dunfee in the big Bentley, with Cyril Paul and John Cobb third in a Sunbeam, despite a broken chassis frame.

The following year the race was run in heavy rain, making life particularly difficult for drivers of the larger cars. Sammy Davis was back, this time paired with the Earl of March in a tiny, works-entered Austin Seven Ulster. This remarkable 750cc car could lap steadily at over 80 mph and despite tough competition from the much faster Bentley of Dr Dudley Benjafield and Eddie Hall, Davis and March came home the winners at 83.41 mph, probably the finest competition result achieved by the baby Austin. Not everyone appreciated the use of handicapping for these important races – some maintained that the winner should be the fastest car overall – but for many enthusiasts the David versus Goliath performances of the smaller cars had a distinct appeal and several manufacturers maintained racing teams, aware of the fine publicity on offer following a good result at the Track.

Opposite:
In 1932 the JCC replaced the double 12 race with a two-day event over 1,000 miles, won by Elsie Wisdom and Joan Richmond in a Riley.

43

John Cobb
at speed, and
airborne in the
Napier-Railton.
This combination
set the fastest ever
lap of the Outer
Circuit in 1935
at 143.44 mph.
The photographers
were either
very brave or
somewhat lacking
in imagination!

In 1930 Colonel Lindsay Lloyd retired and Percy Bradley replaced him as Clerk of the Course. Bradley had been the secretary of the JCC, and one of his first innovations was the introduction of regular mountain racing for the four-wheeled brigade, with a series of short handicap races, usually over ten laps, that provided a good test of acceleration and brakes around the short circuit. The season climaxed with the Autumn Mountain Championship, but although the Mountain Circuit had its fans, for many drivers high speed on the Outer Circuit was still the ultimate test.

John Cobb, who came third in the BRDC '500' in 1929, was a wealthy fur broker who had tasted success in a variety of cars, in particular an ageing 10.5-litre V12 Delage that had been run by the factory in French speed trials in the 1920s. Brought over to Brooklands, the car enjoyed a new lease of life in the hands of drivers like Cobb, Oliver Bertram and the diminutive Kay Petre, who managed to get the big old car around the Outer Circuit at 134.75 mph in 1935. This exploit gained her one of the coveted 130 mph badges, awarded to a select group of drivers, seventeen in all, who lapped the Outer Circuit at more than 130 mph.

With a glance over his shoulder at the aero-engined cars of the early 1920s, Cobb now commissioned Thomson and Taylor to design and build a

Sammy Davis in the 1930 BRDC '500'-winning Austin Seven. The small Austins and MGs regularly performed above expectations in big races at Brooklands.

Malcolm Campbell demonstrating his land speed record-breaking Bluebird at the Track. The cars were developed by Thomson and Taylor at their workshops in the Flying Village. They later built John Cobb's land speed record car.

new aero-engined car capable of taking the world 24 hours record. Reid Railton, the designer, used a Napier 'Lion' aero-engine, a design that dated back to 1919 but was renowned for its rugged reliability. On the test bench it developed 564 bhp from 23,970cc in a W12 cylinder formation.

The chassis was designed for strength, with two massive side-rails under-slung at the rear with twin cantilever springs on each side. As the

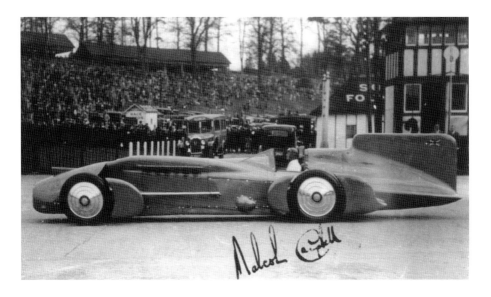

Right: Kay Petre was one of the outstanding competitors at Brooklands in the 1930s. She lapped the Outer Circuit at 135 mph in the 10.5-litre Delage.

Below: The Members' Hill was a delightful venue for spectators when both Mountain and Outer Circuits were in use, with car parking and a restaurant close by.

car was for track use only, braking was only applied to the rear wheels. Special Dunlop treadless tyres were developed especially for the car, and besides record breaking the car seemed tailor-made for the high-speed BRDC 500 miles race.

The resulting Napier-Railton was certainly fast. In 1934 Cobb took the outright lap record from Sir Henry Birkin's Bentley with a speed of 139.71 mph, but wisely withdrew from the BRDC '500' when the track was swamped with heavy rain. The following year Cobb set a new world 24 hours record on the salt flats at Utah, then returned home to win the '500' at 121.28 mph after a duel with Oliver Bertram in the Bentley-based Barnato-Hassan. Bertram had pushed the Outer Circuit record to 142.60 mph and on 7 October

1935 Cobb responded with a run at 143.44 mph on a damp track with the car sliding around enough to use up its tyres in two laps! This great effort was to stand as the outright record for all time.

In 1937 Cobb, now co-driven by Bertram, gave the Napier-Railton its final Brooklands outing and another victory in the final '500' at 127.05 mph. He then turned his attention to the land speed record with another Reid Railton design, constructed at the Track by Thomson and Taylor who had also been responsible for developing Malcolm Campbell's Bluebird record-breaker.

At the other end of the scale, the much smaller MGs from Abingdon were also forging a fine reputation at the Track. Ronnie Horton and Jack Bartlett had won the 1932 '500' in a streamlined single-seater Midget, and the following year Eddie Hall took the race with a K3 Magnette. MGs also set impressive records around the Outer Circuit, with Major A. T. G. 'Goldie' Gardner holding the 1,100cc record at 124.4 mph, and George Harvey Noble lapping at an astounding 122.4 mph in a 750cc derivative of the MG Midget.

For 1933, the ever-innovative JCC had come up with a fresh idea for the new International Trophy Race. The course ran clockwise around the '6 Hours' circuit, running down the Finishing Straight to the Fork, then right onto the Byfleet Banking and along the Railway Straight before returning onto the Finishing Straight. Rather than having handicaps based on time or distance, the club came up with a system of chicanes, graded according to the

Margaret Allen 'flying' Richard Marker's Bentley on the Members' Banking. She lapped at just under 120 mph in this car, a typical Outer Circuit special developed from a touring Bentley.

A BARC car badge showing the Members' Bridge and some typical Weybridge trees. The bridge spanning the famous banking was a trademark image of the Track.

power of the cars. This took advantage of the great expanse of concrete at the Fork, where the track was divided according to engine size. While the smallest cars continued uninterrupted, the larger-engined machines went through different turns, constructed from sand and marked by barrels, which could be altered during practice to achieve a parity of lap times between the different competitors, the largest cars being faced with a virtual hairpin bend.

The first International Trophy Race was won by the Honourable Brian Lewis, driving an Alfa Romeo Monza Grand Prix car after a duel with Malcolm Campbell (V12 Sunbeam), Kaye Don (Bugatti T54), and Whitney Straight (Maserati). Eddie Hall eventually finished second, with Elsie Wisdom following home in third, both in K3 MGs. It was another fine performance from Elsie Wisdom following her win in the previous year's 1,000 miles race. For a long time the BARC had been loath to allow women to compete against men but now finally relented. The smaller clubs like the JCC had been less restrictive for some years and drivers such as Ivy Cummings, Kay Petre, Gwenda Hawkes, Doreen Evans and Jill Scott had already proved themselves the equal of the male competitors around the Track.

Sammy Davis, just after his successful demonstration run in the new BMW 328, where he put over 100 miles into the hour in front of RAC observers.

Away from race weekends, Brooklands was an ideal place for the motor trade to demonstrate interesting machinery to potential customers. On one occasion, the stage comedian Jimmy Nervo of 'Crazy Gang' fame, having shown interest in an Aston Martin on the 1932 Olympia Motor Show stand, was given a high-speed demonstration at the Track that secured his order.

Showbusiness celebrities didn't just visit Brooklands to try out new cars. Several films were made at the Track, including the Will Hay comedy *Ask a Policeman*, which featured a sequence involving a bus travelling against the flow of traffic apparently during a race, while on another occasion, the stark modern architecture of the airfield Clubhouse was transformed into a Middle Eastern setting.

The Track also remained a popular venue for various publicity stunts. In 1936 BMW had introduced its new 328 sports car and the British importers were keen to publicise this advanced new design. H. J. Aldington, the managing director, had already run the car in one of the MCC's high speed trials and covered just over 98 miles during the hour so he decided to demonstrate the new model's potential with an observed run at over 100 mph around the Track. Sammy Davis from *The Autocar* was an obvious choice for the driver and in April 1937, under official RAC observation, he covered just over 102 miles in one hour around the Outer Circuit. At the time very few sporting cars could reach 100 mph in a straight line, so this run in a fully equipped 2-litre road car received very favourable publicity in the press, not least in the pages of *The Autocar*.

A couple of months later BSA made a surprise entry in a three-lap handicap around the Outer Circuit, with a new 500cc motorcycle based on the Empire Star model, but revised and highly tuned. The company

The high speed trials remained popular throughout the 1930s. Here three cars pass the famous Vickers logo on the factory wall opposite the Fork in the late 1930s, with a Vauxhall 30-98 leading the way.

The coveted BMCRC Gold Star was awarded to motorcyclists who lapped the Outer Circuit at over 100 mph during a race.

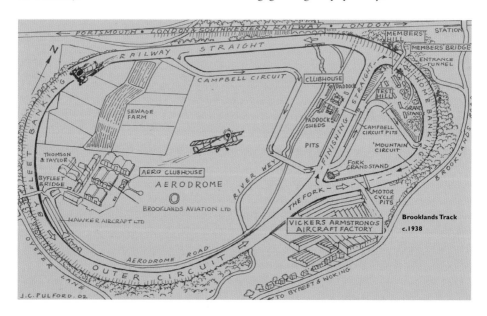

had been out of motor sport since 1921 and in the intervening years its machines had developed a reputation as worthy but dull workhorses. The new machine was entrusted to Wal Handley, a multiple Tourist Trophy winner who had retired from motorcycling in 1934. Handley showed that he had lost none of his skill as he won the race with a fastest lap of 107.57 mph. This earned Handley the BMCRC's Gold Star, a small lapel badge in the form of a six-pointed star, enamelled dark blue with the border and the number 100 in the centre picked out in gold. The BMCRC awarded the star to anyone who completed a lap at Brooklands at over 100 mph during a race, and to honour Handley's achievement, the following year BSA announced a sporting '500' named the Gold Star.

By 1936 Ethel Locke King had been a widow for several years and she decided to sell her shares in the Brooklands Estate Company. Subsequently the Track, and Brooklands House, were taken over by Brooklands (Weybridge) Ltd, with Malcolm Campbell and Percy Bradley among the directors. With road racing growing in popularity, the new owners

Plan of the Track, c. 1938, with the Campbell Circuit completed. The close proximity of Weybridge Station allowed many visitors to reach the Track in the days before mass car ownership.

Brooklands Track c.1938

J.C.PULFORD. 02

Kenneth Evans supervises refuelling of his Tipo B Alfa Romeo Grand Prix car at the Esso pagoda. In later life he did much to help preserve the historic structures at Brooklands.

constructed the 2.26-mile Campbell Circuit (designed by the recently knighted Sir Malcolm), which meandered across the infield from the Railway Straight, crossed the Finishing Straight at an angle, then linked up with the Outer Circuit at the beginning of the Members' Banking. Dame Ethel opened the new circuit in April 1937, and the first race, over 100 laps for the Campbell Trophy, was won by the Siamese Prince Bira driving a Maserati after a duel with Earl Howe's ERA, which was resolved when Howe overturned his car at the bridge over the River Wey.

Pedal power around the Campbell Circuit in 1938. Over the years thousands of cyclists competed at the Track and racing took place long after motor sport had abandoned Brooklands.

A programme for the 1937 JCC International Trophy. The International Trophy was notable for some typical JCC inventiveness relying on a multi-channel chicane at the Fork to provide close racing. In 1937 the race was won by Raymond Mays driving an ERA.

THE
INTERNATIONAL TROPHY
1/- OFFICIAL PROGRAMME

H.J Moser

BROOKLANDS

MONDAY, AUGUST 2nd 1937
START 2-30 P.M. DISTANCE 200 MILES

COPYRIGHT. All literary matter in this Programme, including the Lists of Competitors, is Copyright, and any person found making illegal use thereof will be prosecuted.

Organised by: **THE JUNIOR CAR CLUB.**

Opposite bottom: Real road racing for the motorcyclists at last, as the Campbell Circuit is opened in 1938.

The new road circuit also proved popular with the pedal-powered brigade. Cycling had become a major sport in the late Victorian and early Edwardian era and several Brooklands personalities such as Edge and Roe had been keen competitive cyclists. So it is no surprise to find that a major 100 miles race was held in September 1907, using the Finishing Straight, the Byfleet Banking and the Railway Straight.

Although the cyclists were back in 1910 there were no more competitions at the Track until 1933, when the Charlotteville Cycling Club organised a 100 kilometres world championship trial which used the Outer Circuit, part of the Finishing Straight and, on every third lap, a strenuous excursion involving a climb up the Test Hill with the competitors passing over the Members' Bridge before returning to the Track via the Paddock entrance road.

By the late 1930s the Track – in particular the new Campbell Circuit – was in regular use, with over twenty meetings being held during the year. Indeed, cycle racing was revived from 1969 to the 1980s when a series of charity events used the airfield roads, long after motor sport had ended at the Track.

Apart from the racing, there was still plenty going on at the Track. In 1939 the Ford Motor Company organised a rally and gymkhana for Ford owners, which attracted the largest crowd ever seen at a motoring meeting as the company put on an impressive display of the latest models, along with driving tests and games for enthusiastic Ford owners.

Unfortunately the international situation meant that the BARC's August 1939 race meeting would be the last ever held at the Track. Racing took place on the Mountain, Campbell, and Outer circuits, and was enlivened by a spirited attempt on the Outer Circuit record by Chris Staniland in his Alfa Romeo-based Multi Union. Lapping at 142.30 mph, Staniland came close, but the silver machine was misfiring and John Cobb's October 1935 record would survive for all time.

The 1939 Ford Gymkhana attracted an enormous crowd as the firm demonstrated the latest models, and provided fun and games for enthusiastic owners.

AVIATION ASCENDANT

A T THE OUTBREAK of war in September 1939, Brooklands was requisitioned by the government. Trees were planted on the Banking and elaborate camouflage with netting and paint helped to disguise the Track.

By 1939 Vickers-Armstrong was producing the Rex Pierson-designed Wellington twin-engined bomber in considerable numbers in its factory opposite the Fork. The aircraft was unusual for its geodesic construction method, devised by Barnes Wallis for use in airships, and pioneered by Vickers with the single-engined Wellesley bomber. This was an aluminium alloy lattice structure that enabled the aircraft to withstand severe damage. Most examples used the Bristol Pegasus radial piston engines, although the Bristol Hercules and the Rolls-Royce Merlin engine were also used in some developments. The Wellington was the RAF's front-line bomber in the early years of the war before being replaced by the larger, four-engined heavy bombers such as the Avro Lancaster and Handley Page Halifax. These aircraft were capable of carrying the larger bomb loads now required, including the Tall Boy and 10-ton Grand Slam devised by Barnes Wallis, working in his office in the old Clubhouse, as well as his famous dam-buster 'bouncing bomb'. Wellington production finally ended in early 1943 after 2,515 were built at Brooklands out of a total of over 11,000. The aircraft flew its last offensive sortie over Hannover on 8 October, 1943.

Besides the Wellington, Vickers was also developing the Warwick. Designed in parallel with the Wellington, the Warwick also used Barnes Wallis's geodesic airframe. Larger than the Wellington, but still powered by two engines, the Warwick arrived too late to make an impression as a bomber but was used instead for transport and air-sea rescue roles.

Meanwhile Hawkers (now the Hawker-Siddeley Aircraft Company) had developed the Sydney Camm-designed Hurricane fighter at its factory at Kingston. The aircraft was developed in response to the Air Ministry specification for a fighter aircraft built around a new Rolls-Royce engine, later known as the Merlin. Although Camm's first ideas were considered too conservative, the company persevered privately with a revised design for a

Opposite: Concorde fuselages under construction. More components of this Anglo-French project were manufactured at Brooklands than at any other site, including the fuselage, the nose, and 90 miles of wiring for each aircraft.

An aerial photograph of the Track, taken in 1938, showing the new Campbell Circuit. The notorious sewage farm that ensnared many novice pilots is shown just above the flying village.

monoplane with a retractable undercarriage. To speed development Camm utilised as many existing tools and jigs as possible, and the new aircraft was first testflown at Brooklands in 1935 by George Bulman. It had been apparent for some time that to produce the aircraft in the high numbers envisaged, additional manufacturing facilities would be required, as the Kingston factory was stretched to capacity. A new assembly shop was erected at Brooklands on the site of some of the old flying sheds by the Byfleet Banking, and components produced at Kingston were transported there for final assembly and testing. This continued until Hawker-Siddeley moved production to a new site at Langley, complete with its own airfield, in October 1942, after

Wellington construction in 1939, showing the Barnes Wallis-designed geodesic method of construction. The aircraft was the backbone of Bomber Command in the early years of the Second World War.

3,012 Hurricanes had been built at Brooklands – many of them having taken part in the Battle of Britain.

All aircraft production facilities were a target for the Luftwaffe, and Brooklands was no exception. Following some minor attacks, several Messerschmitt Bf 110s attacked the site in September 1940. They dropped numerous bombs on the Vickers site by the Fork just as workers were returning from lunch, killing 85 and injuring over 400. Wellington production resumed

The finished article being pushed across the River Wey prior to testing. Over 2,500 Wellington bombers were built at Brooklands.

The Vickers factory in 1939. Aircraft had to be pushed over the track to reach the airfield. During the Second World War, elaborate camouflage was used to disguise the site but despite this the factory suffered damage in a severe bombing raid in 1940.

within 24 hours, but at a reduced rate for some time, whilst some sub-assembly work was assigned to smaller workshops scattered around the area.

Following the end of the war, it soon became obvious that motor sport would never return to Brooklands. The major repairs required would have been too costly and, besides, the Air Ministry was reluctant to allow any access to the Track. In 1948 Vickers took over the whole site and Brooklands became a purely industrial area. A large concrete runway was laid down and part of the Byfleet Banking removed.

Although the wartime requirement for military aircraft disappeared virtually overnight, Vickers was able to anticipate a major expansion of civil aviation and produced the Viking (derived from the Wellington but with a stressed-skin fuselage) suitable for short-haul commercial flights. Using Bristol Hercules engines, originally the Viking relied on Wellington-style geodesic wings, although these were soon changed for a stressed-skin design. From this base Vickers developed the Valetta military transport and the Varsity military training aircraft.

The Viking was always seen as a stopgap, although over 160 were built, and in the early 1950s Vickers introduced the Viscount, powered by four

Rolls-Royce turboprop engines, which set new standards for an airliner of its size and proved popular with over forty airlines around the world. Meanwhile the RAF was required to respond to new strategic challenges with a series of fast, high-altitude bombers, capable of carrying nuclear weapons. Vickers developed the Valiant to this specification, powered by four Rolls-Royce Avon turbojets and capable of flying at 600 mph at 50,000 feet. It was the first of the V-bomber force that later included the Handley Page Victor and Avro Vulcan. With a total production run of 100 aircraft, the Valiant saw service during the Suez crisis of 1956, when conventional bombs

A Hawker Hurricane at the Track. This rugged design proved vital during the Battle of Britain, when the RAF prevented the Luftwaffe from preparing the way for a German invasion of the country.

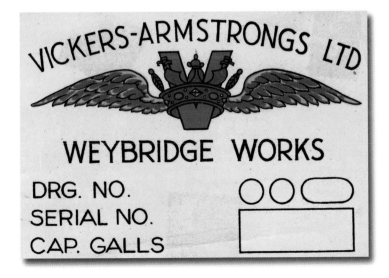

The Vickers logo was respected throughout the world of aviation. This label would have identified a propeller.

The Vickers Viking proved a successful short-haul airliner in the immediate post-war period, securing the future of aircraft manufacture at Brooklands.

The Vickers Valiant was built at Brooklands, then flown out to Wisley for further testing. It was considered necessary to remove a large section of the Byfleet Banking to facilitate a safe take-off.

were dropped on Egyptian airfields. Later the Valiant was adapted as a tanker for air-to-air refuelling and also used for photo-reconnaissance missions before being taken out of service in 1965.

The next large commercial project was the Rolls-Royce Tyne turboprop-powered Vanguard, but the new aircraft had been overtaken by the jet age and sales were disappointing as only forty-three were built. There was a further setback when the TSR2 military aircraft project was summarily cancelled by the government in the 1965 Budget. In the meantime Vickers – since 1960 part of the British Aircraft Corporation (BAC) – had the exciting new VC10 passenger jet in production, and also constructed major components for the BAC One-Eleven, aimed at short-haul carriers. The VC10, with four Rolls-Royce Conway engines fitted at the rear, was a favourite amongst experienced long-distance travellers, but once again failed to meet sales expectations.

There was more to come, as BAC had entered into an agreement with the French company Sud Aviation to design and build the remarkable Concorde supersonic airliner. The Brooklands factory had the distinction of building more of the aircraft than any other site, including the characteristic nose, flight deck and fuselage. Unfortunately, this was the last major aviation project at the site, which was subsequently redeveloped for housing and commercial use, seemingly bringing the Brooklands story to an end.

The VC10 under construction. A radical design that never matched the sales success of its American rivals, the VC10 was popular with long-distance passengers.

EPILOGUE

FOR MANY YEARS the Track lay derelict, but in 1967 William Boddy, the editor of Motor Sport, founded The Brooklands Society, originally with a view to organising reunions for surviving Brooklands *habitués*. As the society grew, members assisted in clearing large areas of the Outer Circuit, and Kenneth Evans (who had competed regularly at Brooklands) worked hard with other volunteers to guarantee the preservation of what remained of the Track and several historic buildings.

In the 1980s, 40 acres – which included most of the Home Banking, the clubhouse, and many of the surviving workshops – were sold to Gallaher Limited for the building of new offices. Subsequently Elmbridge Council, appreciating the heritage and significance of the site, was able to sign a 99-year lease with the company for the key 30 acres that included the historic structures. They subsequently established the Brooklands Museum, based in the clubhouse. Besides many restored buildings and the Home Banking – spanned by a rebuilt Members' Bridge – the Museum also has an interesting collection of vehicles and aircraft linked with the Track that help to introduce new generations to the magic of Brooklands.

Below right:
The Members' Banking today, still a potent reminder of the great deeds carried out here before 1939.

Below:
The Test Hill today. Much of the site has been restored and the museum welcomes thousands of visitors every year.

FURTHER INFORMATION

FURTHER READING

Belton, Gerry. *All the Years at Brooklands*. Centennial Publications, 2007.

Bird, Roger. *A Glimpse of the Vintage Years of Motorcycling at Brooklands*. 2008. (Available from the Brooklands Museum shop)

Boddy, William. *Brooklands: The Complete Motor Racing History*. Motor Racing Publications Ltd, 2002.

Boddy, William. *Brooklands Giants*. Haynes Publishing, 2006.

Davis, S. C. H. 'Sammy' (Ed. Peter Heilbron). *My Lifetime in Motorsport*. Herridge & Sons, 2007.

Mason, David. *Freddie Dixon: The Man with the Heart of a Lion*. Haynes Publishing, 2008.

Pulford, J. S. L. *The Locke Kings of Brooklands Weybridge*. Walton & Weybridge Local History Society, 1996.

Venables, David. *Brooklands: The Official Centenary History*. Haynes Publishing, 2007.

PERIODICALS

The Automobile, Enthusiast Publishing Ltd, PO BOX 153, Cranleigh, GU6 8ZL
Website: www.the-automobile.co.uk

Motor Sport, 38 Chelsea Wharf, 15 Lots Road, London, SW10 0QJ
Website: www.motorsportmagazine.co.uk

CLUBS

Brooklands Museum, Brooklands Road, Weybridge, Surrey, KT13 0QN Telephone: 01932 857381
Website: www.brooklandsmuseum.com

The Brooklands Society
Website: www.brooklands.org.uk

Brooklands Trust Members – the official support organisation for Brooklands Museum
Website: www.brooklandsmembers.co.uk

A visit to Brooklands Museum is highly recommended.

INDEX

Page numbers in italic refer to illustrations